Wicca Love Spells:

Love Magick for the Beginner and the Advanced Witch – Spell Casting Recipes and Potions for Romance

By Kristina Benson

Wicca Love Spells: Love Magick for the Beginner and the Advanced Witch – Spell Casting Recipes and Potions for Romance

ISBN 13: 978-1-60332-019-1

Table of Contents

Introduction

Included herewith is a collection of love spells that I have both written and collected. I have used many of them with great success, and know many others who also have been pleased with the results.

The book assumes that you know the basics of spellcasting and the Craft in general. It is assumed that you know how to cast a circle, take a ritual bath, purify talismans and crystals, and find or make suitable ointments and oils. It is also important that you have learned the basics of visualization and meditation, and can take into consideration all Astrological implications, energy currents and Moon phases.

For all spells, but particularly these, it is crucial that you are very clear about what you want, and why you want them. It is, at the very least, not nice to cast a spell on an unknowing person and cause him or her harm and, and your harmful actions can in turn bring about threefold bad karma. To avoid this, examine your reasons for wanting to cast a spell and know exactly what outcome it is you are looking for.

Additionally important when casting these spells is to engage in some deep mediation and reflection to figure out why you are blocked from getting, finding, or keeping your love. Sometimes the problem is with the other person: maybe the one you love has been hurt before and is wary of falling in love again, or is overly preoccupied with work at the expense of time for him or herself. Sometimes, however, the problem lies only with you, and it is important to critically examine what you could be doing to repel the very one you want to attract.

Before deciding on which basic love spell to use in your quest for love, go through the necessary ritual bath and consecration process. If, for some reason, you find yourself unable to prepare with a ritual bath, make sure at least to wash your hands thoroughly and rinse the negative energy from your skin.

The most important component of success, however, is to know that a spell is given its strength through the sheer power of your mind. You must believe in the spell you are casting and you must concentrate in order to successfully find love.

Though you will find similarities between some of the spells, each working should be highly individualized, personal, and charged with energy. Magick, remember, can be thought of as a manipulation of energy. Do not scatter your energy by attempting to do more than one magickal working at a time, and remember to open your heart and your mind to love.

May you find the love you are looking for!

A Note on Ingredients

If at all possible, ingredients and components of spells and potions should be fresh and organic. I say "organic" because I feel that it's important to know that no negative energy or suffering was created in order to produce a given ingredient. I try to make sure that the fabrics I use are not made in countries that use sweatshop labor and that there were no pesticides used in the cultivation of my herbs and teas. Making your own candles and growing your own herbs are, of course, ideal, but if this is not feasible, then just try to select the best quality ingredients.

When the spell calls for paper, it is best to use high quality parchment, or, if this is not possible, to try to find paper that is free of acids and bleach. Some even advocate using paper from grocery bags. I generally prepare my paper by folding it over a consecrating athame, and then tearing it carefully along the lines. If you must use scissors, use scissors that are only for Magickal purposes.

All tools should be consecrated before use, even if the spells don't explicitly call for you to do so. If a tool has fallen into the wrong hands, or even been touched by anyone else, cleanse and charge it thoroughly before using it in magic.

Also, some spells ask you to drink a potion or use it as a salve. As always, when using an exotic herb or ingredient that you have never ingested, use caution, and stay away from any known allergens.

A Note About Safety

Many of these spells call for the use of flame. They ask you to light candles, let them burn down, or burn things. It is important to pay close attention to any lit candle. Candles are responsible for over 10,000 residential fires per year, according to the Boulder, Colorado fire chief.

A fire extinguisher can be purchased for a relatively low price at most hardware stores. Make sure you read the directions and understand how to use it before you put yourself in a situation where you may need it.

Long robes, billowy sleeves, and long hair can easily catch fire. If your robe catches fire, remember to stop, drop, and roll. Hair burns very quickly and smells awful. Once it's gone, it's gone, so be very careful if you have long hair.

Don't leave a candle unattended, and if you are asked to let a candle burn down, make sure it is on a non-flammable surface, such as a silver or porcelain plate. Don't permit pets to remain unsupervised in a room with a burning candle, and especially be careful to keep lit candles from the reach of children.

Remember, keep a fire extinguisher handy, or at least a pail of water, and watch the candle!

WICCAN LOVE SPELLS

Love Spell #1: Banishing Negative Energy

Necessary Materials:
Candles and oils for ritual bath

You may want to do this spell as preparation for any other love spell you do. After taking a ritual bath, sit quietly and enter a meditative state.

Look inside yourself: is there something in you that blocks love? For instance, do you feel you don[1]t deserve love? Or are you so afraid to open your heart that you push everyone away and say that that no one deserves you?

Think of the negativity that surrounds your heart. Visualize yourself surrounded by black static. Take another ritual bath and visualize the water washing away the negative energy, and facilitating your ability to find love.

Love Spell #2: The Path to Love

Necessary Materials:
Five red roses

Pick (or purchase) five red roses.

Take your ritual bath.

Take your roses, leave your house, and after walking a block or so, drop a rose.

Go another block, and drop another rose.

Return home, and drop two more on the way.

Leave the fifth at your door.

As you do this, chant to yourself:

> *This is a path of love*
> *So may my true love find me.*

Love Spell #3: The Peacock Spell

Necessary materials:
Peacock feather, or decorative feather, or emblem of a peacock.

This spell is primarily to assist you in feeling confidant. Put on your feather or emblem. The emblem can be daring, such as wearing an entire dress with a peacock pattern, or subtle, such as wearing a small peacock pin.

Wear this as you go about your daily business. Think about the peacock, and his pride. Meditate on his energy. Wear the emblem until you feel confidant enough to carry yourself with pride.

Love Spell #4: The Braid Spell

Necessary Materials:
Three pink cords or strings

Take three pink cords or strings and braid them tightly together. Firmly tie a knot near one end of the braid, thinking of the love you have to share.

Next, tie another knot, and another, until you have tied seven knots. Wear or carry the cord with you until you find your love.

After that, keep the cord in a safe place, or sacrifice it to one of the elements- burn and scatter the ashes, throw the cord into a lake or the ocean, or bury it.

Love Spell #5: Spell To Ease a Broken Heart

Necessary Materials:
Dried peach leaves
wand
2 pink candles
a mirror
one drawstring bag
one quartz crystal
one bowl
1 teaspoon dried jasmine
1 tsp. strawberry leaves
1 teaspoon dried lavender
10 plus drops apple-blossom oil
10 plus drops strawberry oil

Take your ritual bath with dried peach leaves, and pink candles. When you emerge, cast your circle, and light a new pink candle. Mix all oils and herbs in the bowl. Stir them counterclockwise three times, and then look in the mirror and say:

> *I honor the Goddess/God within me.*
> *My love has gone*
> *But others will come*
> *So mote it be.*

Then put half the mixture in the bag and add the penny and the crystal. Carry it with you until your heart has healed. Leave the other half of the potion in the bowl in your bedroom. Whenever you catch its scent, say to yourself that you honor the Goddess within yourself.

Repeat whenever necessary.

Love Spell #6: Desire Spell

Necessary Materials:
Red candle
Musk oil

This spell is best done when the moon is waxing, and should ideally be performed sky-clad.

First, take a ritual bath to the light of a red candle. When you emerge, visualize your name and his name on a new red candle.

Dress the candle with musk oil, and then say:

> *Goddess of love*
> *God of fire*
> *Make his heart*
> *For me desire.*

Now close your eyes, and enter a meditative state. Focus on the man you desire, and imagine him touching you. Let the candle burn all the way down, and only rise when it has snuffed itself out.

Love Spell #7: Attraction Spell

Necessary Materials:
Ginger
Rosemary
Rose petals
Violet
Lavender
Pink candle
Bowl

This spell is not designed to attract anyone specific; it is merely a spell to make you seem more attractive to the one you are meant to be with, even if you don't yet know him/her.

Take your ritual bath, and cast a circle. Gather the herbs you will need. They can be dried but fresh herbs are more potent. Light the pink candle and mix the herbs together in the bowl. As the candle burns, say:

> *My lover true I may not know*
> *Reveal him to me*
> *So that him/her I may know.*
> *My true love's face I want to see*
> *May the Goddess reveal his/her face to me.*

Let the candle burn down, making sure you supervise it,
and leave the herbs in the bowl overnight.

Love Spell #8: Bath Love Spell

Necessary Materials:
Peach, rose, strawberry, or lavender essential oils
Pink candles
Clean towel, preferably white or pink

Dress at least two pink candles in essential oil. Then draw a bath, and scent it with the oil, and a few petals of a flower, if you wish. Place white or pink candles around the tub.

As you warm in the water visualize the person, or type of person, you wish to attract. As you do so, meditate on the following:

> *Many heads will turn my way*
> *the ones I choose will wish to stay.*

Complete your bath, dry off, and meditate briefly on what you want.

Love Spell #9: Spell to Color a Relationship

Necessary materials:
One red candle
One pink candle
One white candle
One brown candle
One blue candle
Chalk, lipstick, or marker
Table or other surface

Draw a Pentagram on your table, or even on the floor if you wish, and set the candles on the five points of the Pentagram. Place a bowl of water in the middle.

Light all the candles. Red is for passion; pink for romantic love; white is for spiritual or intellectual; brown is for friendship; blue is for nurturing. Pull five hairs from your head. Twist the hairs together and press them to the melted candle wax of whatever color represents the types of qualities you want in your relationship, to the candle that bears the color of your chosen kind of relationship.

Then take the chosen candle and stir the water in the bowl five times. Place the candle by your bed.

Every night, light the candle and say:

> *Light of stars, light of moon,*
> *My lover will to me come soon.*
> *I see the morning light*
> *I will dream of him/her tonight.*

Do this each night, and stop when you dream of the one you want. Contact him or her, and he will be receptive.

Love Spell #10: Egyptian Musk Spell
(note: this one is only to be performed by women).

Materials Needed:
Honey
Plum wine
Cinnamon
Cloves

This one is derived from an Egyptian love spell.

First, shave your armpits, genitals, and legs, and then take a ritual bath. After your bath, boil together honey, plum wine, cinnamon and cloves to create a decoction. Let it cool somewhat. Then dip the ring finger of your left hand in the warm decoction and spread a small quantity of the mixture between the inner lips of your labia major. Refrain from masturbation until the spell has worked its magic.

Make and apply the decoction daily until your lover returns to your bed.

Love Spell #11: Fire Spell

Materials Needed:
Rosemary
Two rose petals
Dried ginseng

Take a ritual bath, and cast a circle. In the middle of the circle, light a fire, if possible, and cast into it a pinch or rosemary, two rose petals, and the ginseng. If you cannot safely light a fire, simply surround a bowl with red candles, and throw the ingredients in the bowl.

Chant the name of the one you love until the candles or fire burns out.

Love Spell #12: Gypsy Love Spell

Materials Needed:
Tulip or daffodil bulb
Needle
Marker

Write the name of your beloved on the onion or the garlic bulb. Plant the bulb in a red clay pot, in fertile soil. Prick your finger and put a drop of the blood in the pot.

Tend to the plant at sunset every day and say:

> *As grows this root*
> *So does (lover's name) love.*

If the plant dies, you are not meant to have the person you want.

Love Spell #13: Gypsy Willow Knot Spell

(This spell should only be performed by men).

Necessary materials:
Willow twigs

To win the favor of a lady, a man must seek out willow trees whose branches have grown into a knot. This must be done on midsummer's eve. With a sharp knife with a white handle he must cut the twigs, put them in his mouth, and repeat the following with his eyes closed:

> *"Willow tree, Willow Tree*
> *Give me the luck of thine,*
> *Then (her name) shall forever be mine."*

Make sure you spit out the twigs. Also, white willow bark is known to be a natural painkiller, and cures headaches.

Love Spell #14: To Bring A Lover Back

Necessary Materials:
Paper
Red candle
Pen

Take your ritual bath, and when you emerge, light the red candle. Write on the paper:

> *If your heart still aches for me*
> *know that my heart aches the same*
> *with this candle, I rekindle the flame*
> *By the Goddess, so mote it be.*

Then write the name of the person on the paper three times. Once you have finished, burn the paper in the flame of the red candle. Say the above verse again.

Love Spell #15: The Spell of Nine

Necessary Materials:
Pink candle
Rosewater
Honey
Pink silk

For best results, cast this spell at nine o'clock in the evening when the moon is in Taurus. It will make a man/woman desire you.

Take your ritual bath, and then write the name of your beloved nine times, along with yours on a pink candle.

Dress the candle in rosewater and honey. Then light the candle and let it burn for nine minutes every night at nine o'clock for nine nights.

On the ninth night after the candle has been extinguished, wrap it in a pink piece of silk and bury it.

Love Spell #16: Scottish Love Spell

Necessary Materials:
Ivy leaf

Take your ritual bath and then hold an ivy leaf to your breast and say:

> *"Ivy leaf, I love you true*
> *in my heart I hold you.*
>
> *A young man one day will smile at me*
> *true beloved he will be."*

Love Spell #17: To Make A Man Love You

Necessary Materials:
A red rose
White silk

On Midsummer's Eve pick a red rose, then wrap into white silk. Keep it until Yule. Open the silk. If the rose is still intact, carry it with you. The first person who admires it will be your beloved.

Love Spell #18: Indian Spell To Attract A Wealthy Husband

Necessary Materials:
Turmeric oil

Every day for five days, after a bath, anoint yourself with turmeric oil.

Love Spell #19: Witch Candle Spell

Necessary Materials:
Pink candle
Red foil or paper
Rose, peach, strawberry, or patchouli oil.
Pen

On Friday evening, take a ritual bath, and dress a pink candle with rose, peach, strawberry, or patchouli oil. Write the name of your beloved on the candle, light it.
Say three times

> *Candle candle gift of fire*
> *Flame the heart of the man/woman I desire.*

Allow the candle to burn down one centimeter, and wrap the candle in the foil. Repeat nightly until it has burned all the way down. Then, wrap it in foil again, and place it under your bed for seven days and nights. After that, throw it in the ocean, a lake, or a river, and say three times:

> *Candle candle flames to fan*
> *Bring me my desired man/woman.*

Love Spell #20: Modern Photo Spell

Necessary materials:
Picture of you
Picture of beloved
Rose petals
Candle the color of your love's favorite color
Pink candle for ritual bath
Pink or white cloth

Take your ritual bath by the light of the pink candle. When you emerge, take both pictures, and stand them against the candle that is your beloved's favorite color. Scatter rose petals around the candle, preferably pink but red and white are ok too.

Chant or sing the name of your intended until you feel that your energy has locked in with his or hers.

Meditate and imagine the two of you together. Blow out the candle, wrap it in the cloth with the rose petals, and place under your bed for as long as it takes.

Love Spell #21: Spell To Bring Back An Unfaithful Lover

Necessary Materials:

Elfwart root

Orange peel

Amber oil

Red candle

Red ink

Paper

Box

Straw poppets

Lock of hair

Box

Seven red cords or strings

On midsummer's day, make two dolls of straw or corn husk. It's ok if they don't look fantastic; the important thing is that they can function as an effigy. If your arts and crafts skills are too lacking to make a straw poppet, that's ok too. Cut out a male and a female figure from a piece of cardboard and use those.

In the evening, take your ritual bath. When you emerge, take the elfwart root and mix it with orange peel and amber oil in a bowl. Light a red candle, and write your lover's name on a piece of paper using red ink. Burn the paper in the light of the candle, and mix the ashes in with the amber, orange, and elfwart. Place the ashes in a small box along with a lock of your hair and the hair of your beloved. Tie seven red strings with seven tight knots around the box. Place the box under your bed for seven days and seven nights, then anonymously mail it to the unfaithful lover. This will cause him or her to return to you within seven days.

Make sure that no one touches the poppets before you beloved does. This is a very, very powerful spell and you may want to cast a protection spell first, just in case harm befalls the poppets.

Love Spell #22: Santerian Love Spell

Necessary materials:
Yellow candle
Pen
Picture of beloved
Fishhooks
Honey
Dish or bowl

Take your ritual bath, and when you emerge, light the yellow candle. As you do so, say:

> *My beloved that I love so*
> *Let too his love for me grow.*

Place a picture of your intended in a dish. Arrange five fishhooks around the picture and dribble a little bit of honey over the fishhooks. Taste the honey, and visualize you and your beloved together.

Love Spell #23: Sour Love Mirror Spell

Necessary materials:
Photo of the one who broke your heart
Flower pot
Black tea

Place the photo of your intended on the mirror, and then shatter the mirror. Plant the shards in a flower pot, and place the pot on a window. Every Friday sprinkle the earth with black tea, and say the name of your ex lover five times as you do so. Do this for a month. He will know the pain he caused you.

Love Spell #24: Circle Of Light Spell

Necessary materials:
Five white candles
Strawberry or Jasmine oil
Jasmine incense
Picture of beloved

On the night when the moon is in its waxing phase anoint five white or yellow candles with strawberry or jasmine oil.

Sit on the floor, and place the candles in a circle around you.

Place the photo of your beloved in front of you. Say:

> *Five candles for my beloved burn*
> *My love for him/her will be returned.*
> *Goddess great, bring his love to me*
> *As you will, so will it be.*

Gaze into the photo and sing or chant the name of your intended. Remain in the circle until the candles have burned down, and leave the wicks at his or her door step.

Love Spell #25: Spell To Make A Man Desire Only You

Necessary materials:
Red candle approximately six inches long
Hair or fingernail clippings of beloved
Rose petals

Take your ritual bath and scatter rose petals in the water. On the first night of a full moon, put the fingernail clippings or hair into the candle's melted wax. When the wax is cool enough to handle, solid but malleable, say these words:

> *I thank the Goddess as I must*
> *Quench my passion and my lust.*

Once the candle has hardened use it in any way you wish to aid you in fantasizing about your beloved.

Love Spell #26: Venus Love Spell To Return A Lover

Necessary materials:

Silver pin

Red candle

On a Friday night when the waxing moon is in Taurus or Libra put a silver pin through the wick of the candle.

Visualize your lover returning.

Say:

> *Light of Goddess light above*
> *Give him back to me to love.*

Love Spell #27: Spell To Dream Of Your Future Beloved

Necessary materials:

Twig from an ash tree

Take a twig from an ash tree.

Before you go to bed, say:

> *Ashen tree, ashen tree,*
> *tonight my love I want to see.*

Put the sprig under your pillow when the moon is full and you will dream of your future beloved.

Love Spell #28: Apple Spell

Necessary materials:
Red apple
Silver pin

On the night of the new moon, take a red apple and prick it full of holes as you recite your intended's name. Place it on your altar for the night. In the morning, wash, peel and core the apple. Feed it to your intended, and he will love you. You can make it into a pie or bread or applesauce or give it to him plain and raw.

Love Spell #29: Passion spell

Necessary materials:
Apple
Red Candle
Jasmine incense cone
Orange oil

This is for the two of you to do together to magnify the passion you have for each other.

Dress a candle in orange oil, and light it.
Prick your fingers and let a drop of each fall on the incense cone. Say:

> *"Blood of (your name), Love of (your name)"*

And then he/she says:

> *"Blood of (his/her name), Love of (his/her name)"*

Light the incense and pass a red apple through the smoke three times. With a consecrated athame, cut the apple in half. Eat one half and give the other to your lover. The spell takes effect immediately.

Love Spell #30: Reverse Love Spell

Necessary Materials:
White candle
White silk
Pen

This can reverse a love spell that has been cast, or can simply reverse someone's feelings even if no spell was cast. This should be performed during a waning moon.

Write the person's name on the side of the white candle. Light it, and say:

> *This candle burns away your love*
> *So mote it be by the Goddess above.*

Allow the candle to burn out. When the wax has cooled, wrap it in white silk and throw it into the sea or a river.

Love Spell #31: Ritual Love Spell

Necessary materials:

1 teaspoon basil

1 teaspoon marjoram

1 teaspoon whole cloves

five rose petals

red fabric

red thread

silver needle

rose quartz

jasmine or rose incense

This spell is intended to attract a person who will be compatible with you.

Take your ritual bath, and cut two squares out of the fabric. Place your materials on the altar, and light the incense. Cast a circle. Then place the two squares of fabric together, and sew around three sides of the square. Place the squares on the altar and state the purpose of the spell aloud in your own words—what you want, and who you want.

(continued on next page)

Take up the fabric square and turn it right side out. Spoon
the herbs into the bag one at a time saying aloud the
appropriate line as you add each one:

> *"Basil, sacred herb of Mars,*
> *bring to me the love I seek.*
> *Cardamom, sacred herb of Venus,*
> *bring to me the love I seek.*
> *Marjoram, sacred herb of Mercury,*
> *bring to me the love I seek.*
> *Cloves, sacred herb of Jupiter,*
> *bring to me the love I seek.*
> *Rose, sacred flower of Venus,*
> *bring to me the love I seek.*
> *Rose Quartz, stone of peace and love,*
> *Bring to me the love I seek.*

Take up the needle and thread and sew up the last side of
the bag. When you finish, visualize love surrounding you
and wrapping you in a pink mist.

(continued on next page)

Hold the bag and will the energy into it, saying:

> *"I invest this amulet of love*
> *with the power of my vision.*
> *It will bring me the love I desire.*
> *As I will, so mote it be!"*

Dismiss the circle and carry the amulet bag with you at all times.

Love Spell #32: White Candle Love Spell

Necessary materials:
White candle
Pen
Rose thorn
White silk

Prepare an altar and cast your circle.

Using a rose thorn from a white rose bush, inscribe the words "All my love come to me" 3 times on the candle.

Place the inscribed candle in the center of the altar and light it. For the entire time the candle burns, gaze upon it and visualize a pink, loving mist surrounding you.

When the candle burns out, collect the wax puddle that remains, and wrap it in white silk.

You will receive all the love that person has for you. This could be more love than you want, or not enough. If at some future time you no longer wish to receive that person's love, bury the wax at a crossroads.

Love Spell #33: Honey Love Spell

Necessary materials:
a jar of honey
a piece of paper
a pen
a candle (pink or red)

This magic spell can be worked on anyone whose feelings you want to sweeten. It can be used for romance, or to get a boss to favor you, or to get a teacher to give you a better grade.

After you emerge from a ritual bath, cast a circle. Fold your paper into a square, and write the person's name on it three times, one on top of the other thusly:

His/her name
His/her name
His/her name.

Then rotate the paper 90 degrees and write your own name across the person's name, also three times. When you finish, the two names are crossed over each other, like a cross or a tic-tac-toe grid, and the other person's name will be under yours.

Now, all around the crossed names write your specific wish in a circle. Write it in cursive, with no spaces between the words, and make sure you dot your "i's" and cross the T's after you finish writing the circle. This way, you will have written the wish without lifting up the pen. If you make a mistake -- for instance, if you lift your pen or misstate your desired outcome--throw away the paper and start it all over again.

Fold the paper toward you to bring what you want your way and speak aloud your wish as you do so. Turn the paper and fold it again, and again, folding toward you, to bring what you want your way. Speak aloud your wish each time you fold the paper toward you. Fold it until it will not fold any more.

Open the jar of honey. Eat a spoonful and say:

> *"As this honey is sweet to my tongue,*
> *so will I be sweet to (Name of Person).*

Push the folded paper packet down into the jar and close up the lid."

Dress a candle of the appropriate color with the appropriate oil. Since this is a love spell, use a red or pink candle and anoint with rose oil.

Stand the candle on the lid of the closed-up jar and light it. You can melt the candle to the lid with hot wax if need be. Let the candle burn all the way out, or down to the nub. If it puts itself out, this is ok too. Do this every Monday, Wednesday, and Friday, for as long as it takes. Add each new candle on top of the remains of the last one.

Love Spell #34: Easy Candle Love Spell

Necessary Materials:
1 pink candle
1 bottle of 100% Virgin Olive oil

Take your ritual bath, and when you emerge, take the candle and place it on a table or your altar. Now dress the candle in the olive oil. While doing so, visualize love energy flowing from your heart, down your hands, and into the candle. After the oil is finished, take a knife and carve the name of the person you desire into the candle. When you finish writing in the candle, simply light it and meditate on love until the candle has burnt out. Once the candle has burned out, the spell is finished.

Love Spell #35: Attract Love Spell

Necessary Ingredients:
A blank sheet of paper
Scissors
A small wooden or cardboard box
1/4 cup of dried pink rose petals
2 quartz crystals
A plain silver ring for the finger
A pink candle
Strawberry oil

This needs to be performed after the sun has set.

First, take your ritual bath and cast a circle. Then, charge the objects with your energy by concentrating on the objects and visualizing a love entering the objects. You can think of a pink mist, or pink energy, if you want.

Next, cut out a paper heart. Put two drops strawberry oil on it, and then place the paper in the box. Hold the dried rose petals close to your heart for approximately one minute and visualize love; then put them in the box.

Do the same with the crystals. Hold the ring in your hand
and say:

Goddess above

Send me my love

Then, gently place the ring in the box. Light the candle and
set it to the left of the box. Allow the candle to burn exactly
13 minutes, and then put out the candle with your fingers
or a candle snuffer and close the box. Do not blow the
candle out; snuff it or use your fingers. Repeat the ritual of
the candle burning; leaving the box closed, every evening
until candle has burned down to a height of less than
approximately one inch. On the night this occurs, remove
the ring from the box and wear it on your left hand. Your
love will soon come.

Love Spell #36: Come Hither Spell

Necessary Materials:
Red candle
Rose oil
Jasmine incense
Athame

Annoint the candle with the oil, and carve the name of the person you love, using a consecrated athame. Light the incense, and then candle. Burn candle once a day for ten minutes, only after the sun has gone down, until the candle is gone. While doing so visualize what you want to happen.

If you think that you need more power you can add musk oil to the candle. Also, you can do this spell every day until you get the desired outcome.

Love Spell #37: Unlocking Spell

Necessary Materials:
Jasmine incense
Red candle
Black candle
Key
A foot of red lace ribbon

On the night of a full moon, sit before your altar and light the incense and the candles. While meditating on your wish, hold the key in your left hand and say:

> *In this hand I hold the key*
> *To unlock my heart, my soul, and me.*
> *Unlock my heart*
> *So mote it be.*

Then take the key, hang it on the ribbon and wear it around your neck. Snuff out the candle. You may stop wearing the key when you find your love.

Love Spell #38: Grapefruit Love Spell to Find Your Spouse

Necessary Materials:

Grapefruit

On a Friday morning, peel a grapefruit immediately after waking.

Eat the fruit, and keep two equal pieces of the peel.

Place the pieces with the insides together and the peel sides out, and keep them in your breast pocket, or your purse. Leave them there all day. At night, when you undress for bed, rub the peel on the legs of your bed. Then place both pieces of the peel under your pillow and lay down to sleep.

If you dream of your love, then you will surely marry him/her.

Love Spell #39: Reflection Love Spell

Necessary Materials:
Red candle
Hand mirror
Red twine or red cord

On a full moon, at midnight, place the candle on the altar and light it. Hold the mirror to charge it with energy. Then hold the mirror behind the candle and position it so that the flame is reflected onto your face. Say:

> *The light of love shines in my face*
> *The light of love shines in my eyes*
> *The light of love shines in my soul*

Repeat it five times, and then tie five knots in the thread.

Tie the thread around the candle.

Do this every day at midnight until you get your goal.

Love Spell #40: Isis Love Spell

Necessary materials:
Chalice
Plum wine
Red candle
Honey
Raisins

This spell will invoke the Goddess Isis, and her powers.

Set up your altar with gifts with of honey, wine, and raisins.
Say:

> *Isis Isis Goddess great*
> *I need your help to make my fate*

Tell her what you want, even if it doesn't necessarily
involve love. After you have finished, eat the raisins, a
spoonful of the honey, and the wine.

Love Spell #41: Unbinding Spell

Necessary Materials:
Black candle
Picture of you and the star crossed lover together
Scissors

When you know your lover is not the right person for you, try the following ritual to ease the pain of separation.

Cast this spell at a time when the moon is waning. Burn a black candle. Take a picture in which you both are together and cut it in the middle. Then burn the image of the other person. When you do it, say:

Fire light, fire bright, separate our souls tonight.

Take the ashes to the wind, and let them fly away. Keep your part of the picture for a future love spell, when you will be ready to attract the right person into your life.

If this doesn't take care of it all in one go, repeat.

Love Spell #42: Dragon Love Spell

Necessary Materials:

A small wooden disk approximately 3 inches in diameter

The lovers card from a deck of tarot

glue

musk oil

jasmine incense

One pink candle (to attract a woman) or blue (to attract a man)

Rose quartz chip necklace or 9 rose quartz crystals

Red or pink bag big enough to hold the finished disk

Gold fabric paint (or gold paint pen)

Athame

The day before you plan to do the ritual, you should glue the picture from the tarot card onto the disk and allow to dry.

On the day you will be doing the spell, gather all the required items and set up your altar. Then take a ritual bath. When you emerge and are clad in ritual wear (or sky clad), go to your altar.

Inscribe the candle with a heart, using a consecrated athame.

Anoint the candle with the oil while concentrating on bringing the perfect lover and partner into your life. Then, light the candle, and light the incense. Take a moment to concentrate and gather your energy. Then, take the wooden disk and anoint it with the oil. Pass the disk through the incense smoke and over the candle flame while chanting nine times:

> *Lovers, lovers entwined in flight,*
> *Bring to me a love tonight!*

Set the disk down in front of the candle and place the rose quartz on top of it. Repeat the above chant again 5 times while visualizing love energy coming from the rose quartz and being absorbed by the disk. After you feel it has been absorbed, take the bag and paint it with the heart you carved on to the candle.

When it is dry, put the disk inside it. Carry it with you until you find your love. Wait by the altar until the candle has burned down to half its original size.

To charge the bag and disc with your energy, hold it and

repeat the Lover's Chant five times just before you go anywhere.

Repeat the spell once a month on a Friday for as long as you like.

Love Spell #43: Flower love Spell

Necessary Materials:

Sheet of paper
Pen
Daisy petals
Rose incense
Pink or Red candle
Rose quartz
Strawberry oil

Take a ritual bath with a few drops of strawberry oil. When you emerge, dress the candle in more strawberry oil. When finished, light the candle and incense and relax completely. Write down all of the qualities you would like in a mate. When finished with the list, stare at the candle. Holding the daisy petals and gemstones in your hands, visualize the candlelight infusing the items in your hands with energy. Say:

> *Candle candle burning bright,*
> *Help me find my love to night*
> *Make my lover one with me*
> *The goddess wills, so mote it be!*

Sprinkle the petals around the base of the candle, and place the gemstones in front of it. Repeat each month until true love finds you.

Love Spell #44: Braid Love Spell

Necessary Materials:
Pink cord
Red cord
White cord

Braid the three cords together. Then, tie five knots in it. Keep it with you at all times until you find your true love.

Love Spell #45: To Gain Love

Necessary Materials:
Cauldron, bowl, or goblet
Red candle
Two pink candles
Wand

Take a ritual bath. When you emerge, go to your altar and place your cauldron in the middle. Then put the pink candles on either side. Next, put the red candle in the cauldron. Tap the cauldron five times with your wand. Say:

> *I give my love and thus it's thine;*
> *I take your love and so it's mine.*
> *Lover, lover, I am true*
> *In my heart, there is only you.*

Tap the cauldron three more times with the wand. Light the red candle to energize the spell. Let it burn completely down. Repeat whenever necessary.

Love Spell #46: Enchanted Apple Spell

Necessary Materials:
Green apple
Red apple
Athame
Pink cloth

This must be performed during a waxing moon. Pick or select a green apple and a red apple. Cut both in half with a consecrated athame. Take half of the green apple and join it with half of the red apple.

Hold them together and wrap them in the cloth. Breathe on the cloth, and say:

> *Apple green*
> *Apple red,*
> *Warm the heart,*
> *And turn the head. "*

Eat the apple and meditate on what you want to happen. Perform it every Friday evening until you get your wish.

Love Spell #47: Nine White Roses Love Spell

Necessary Materials:
Nine white roses
red food coloring.
Vase with water

Perform this spell on a new moon for best results.

Ready your altar with the roses and a vase. When you emerge from your ritual bath, place the roses in the vase. Add five drops of red food coloring to the water.

Cup your hands around the flowers and inhale deeply the scent of the roses. Say and repeat three times:

> *Roses white will now turn red*
> *Change his heart and turn his head.*

Leave the roses on your altar until they wither. Repeat spell as often as necessary.

Love Spell #48: Dragon Love Spell

Necessary Materials:
Seven small stones
Rose petals
Apple seeds
Rose Quartz

Gather your seven small stones and place them in a circle. In the middle of the circle, scatter a handful of rose petals and apple seeds. Place a rose quartz directly in the middle of the circle. Chant the following:

> *"Roses and apples*
> *Dragons and stone*
> *Bring me my love*
> *So I won't be alone.*
> *Mist of the Dragon*
> *Breath of the night*
> *Draw from the sky*
> *True love that is right."*

Meditate and visualize what you want to happen. When finished, place the stones, petals, and seeds on your altar for at least a week.

Love Spell #49: Rekindle the Fire

2 Fig Cookies
1 heart shaped cookie cutter
A small knife
Vanilla extract
Red candle
Jasmine incense.

The spell is done with two people.

Each of you should take a fig cookie and cut it into the shape of a heart. Carve his/her initials in one cookie and he will carve your initials into the other.

Anoint each other's cookie with the vanilla extract using your thumbs. Light the candle and burn the incense.

Eat each others cookies by crossing arms with each other and gazing into each others eyes.

For best results, accompany the cookies with plum wine.

Love Spell #50: Friendship Candle Spell

Necessary Materials:
Red candle
Yling Ylang oil
Red silk ribbon

After you emerge from your bath, go to your altar and anoint your candle with the oil. As you do so, think of the friends that you want to make and the friendships you'd like to strengthen.

After your candle has been anointed, you may light it. At this point you may list aloud the things that are important to you in a friend. As you watch the candle, focus in on the flame and envision the flame shining good energy on you and your friends. The flame being the energy that burns between any two close friends.

When this is completed, take two pieces of silk ribbon and wind them together. While you do this, think of bringing your friends closer to you. Envision yourself sending more good energy to all of your friends and well-wishers.

Once you have done this, tie the ribbon to the base of your candle. Then sit and meditate on the spell that you have just cast, sending your energies out to bring your friends to you. When you feel that your spell has been completed, then it has. Let your candle burn all the way out and dismiss your circle, thanking the Goddess and the God.

Love Spell #51: Salve for a Wounded Heart

Necessary Ingredients:

New sponge
Pink candle
Rose petals
Almond oil
Honey
Jasmine oil
Bowl of spring water

Take the sponge in your right hand. Sit quietly and think about the relationship you have just ended, and your feelings about splitting up. Really allow yourself to cycle through every emotion—anger, resentment, sadness. Take as long as you want to stew and simmer and think.

When you have been doing this for awhile, and start to wind down, take the sponge and dip it in the water. Pass it gently over your face and forehead. Imagine that the sponge will soak up your grief, your need, and all the negative emotions. Project all your unhappiness over the relationship into the sponge and let it soak up all your negative feelings.

When you have completed this undertaking, bury it. Try not to bury it on your property. Ideally it should be buried at a crossroads.

Return to your house, preferably to your own bedroom or some place where you spend a lot of time. Annoint yourself with the almond oil, and prepare a cup of hot water with honey. Sprinkle the rose petals around the candle and yourself, and light the candle. Imagine the warmth of the candle and the scent of the rose petals combining and filling the room with warmth, sweet rose scent and soft pink light. Let the pink light and scent fill you with loving warmth and comfortable feelings. Say:

> *Water hot and water wet*
> *Let my heart the pain forget*

As you sip the hot water with the honey. Imagine yourself surrounded by a loving pink mist. Gaze into the candle flame and imagine all of the things you can do with your time now that you are no longer with your ex. Imagine yourself taking a dance class, learning to crochet, or having time to plant a garden.

Sit as long as you need, and blow out the candle when you are finished.

Love Spell #52: To Reunite Parted Lovers

Necessary materials:
Silver needle
White stone
Red cloth
Pink ribbon
Pink candle

When the moon is full, light your pink candle. Prick the tip of your left index finger with a sterilized pin or needle. Squeeze out a bit of blood and write your initials, and your lovers' initials on the surface of a smooth white stone. Pass it through the flame of the candle three times, being careful not to burn yourself or light your ritual robes. Wrap the stone in a pink or red cloth tied with a pink ribbon. Bury it next to a flower.

If this spell is done correctly you should be reunited with your lover in 3 days.

Love Spell #53: A Little Bit Closer Spell

Necessary materials:
Chalice filled with spring water
Photo of you
Photo of beloved
Pink candle

Put the photos and a candle in a bowl of water, and allow the candle to burn until the water extinguishes it. Visualize your beloved emerging from a thick pink mist. As you do so, anoint yourself with the water from the bowl and say:

> *Night comes and night will go*
> *Water ebbs and water flows*
> *Show the path to my love dear*
> *The path to me is ever clear.*

Say this three times.

Love Spell #54: Love Sachet

Necessary Materials:
Red or pink silk pouch
pink candle
5 white candles
cauldron
jasmine blossoms
paper
pen
sea salt
spring water
wand

Cast a circle, then consecrate it with sea salt and spring water (or sea water if you wish). Call the Goddess and God (optional), and the four elements.

Place the five candles around the circle, at the five points of the pentacle. Place the pink candle in front of you, behind the cauldron, which should be empty.

Light the white candles, calling to the Goddess and the God, then light the pink candle. Write down on a piece of paper what qualities you want.

Place the paper and the jasmine blossoms into the cauldron.

Tap the cauldron three times with your wand. Then take the contents of the cauldron and put them in the pink bag.

Wear the bag around your neck for at least a week. Repeat if necessary.

Love Spell #55: Beauty Spell

Necessary Materials:
A dish full of earth (good soil, not dry, dusty dirt).
A yellow candle
A full-sized mirror
Olive, patchouli, jasmine, or cinnamon essential oil
A small flower pot
A daffodil bulb

Anoint the candle with the essential oil you have chosen. Place it in the center of the dish of earth. Light it and sit down. Hold mirror behind it. Look deeply into the mirror, and concentrate on your reflection. Contemplate what is your inner beauty, and what is your outer beauty? Notice at least five things you like about each, and say them out loud.

Perform this ritual 3 nights in a row. Once the entire candle has burnt down, remove the wax from the dish.

Place the earth from the dish inside a small flower pot and plant a bulb inside it. Water it and care for it so that it grows properly. You will soon find that your beauty will grow, flourish, and shine.

Love Spell #56: To Undo a Love Spell

Necessary Materials:
Piece of paper
Incense of your choosing
Pen
Black candle

Write your name on a piece of paper, and then the name of the other person. Burn the paper in the flame of the black candle. Say:

> *Away from me turn his head*
> *That he may find another bed*

Then scatter the ashes in the ocean, a lake, or a river. If done correctly, the person won't hate you; he'll just lose interest.

Love Spell #57: Healing Spell

Necessary Materials:
yellow candle with holder
rose petals
lavender oil
small garnets
carnelian or turquoise stone
small jar with lid or plastic bag that seals
picture of yourself

This will help ease pain or get rid of a stubborn and persisting condition. You must, of course, make healthy choices, but this spell can really accelerate the rate at which you will heal.

When you emerge from your ritual bath, charge the rose petals, oil and stones with your energy. Sprinkle petals around candle, again visualize your goal. Place the charged garnet stones, the petals and a few drops of oil into a jar or bag. Seal the jar or bag and say:

> *In this bag I place my pain*
> *That I may be of health again.*

As you watch the candle, imagine that the flame is burning your sickness away. Let the candle burn down at least halfway. Rub the bag on the picture of yourself to transfer some of its energy to your image. Carry this jar or bag with you and sniff charged items before eating.

Burn the candle whenever you feel overwhelmed by your disease or condition.

Love Spell #58: Apple Peel Spell

Necessary Materials:
Apple of any color

Peel an apple in a circle, keeping the entire peel in one long thin strip. Then, throw the peel over your left shoulder. If it stays in one piece it will reveal the initial of your one true love.

Then cut the apple and eat it.

Love Spell #59: Spell for Friendship

Necessary Materials:
Pink candle
Athame
Rose quartz
Olive oil

Using your consecrated athame, inscribe a pink candle
with your name, then anoint the rose quartz with olive oil.
Light the candle. Hold the stone in your hand, and
visualize friendships coming your way and a new
relationships forming. Chant three times:

> *Candle candle burning fire*
> *True friendship is what I desire.*
> *Candle pink and candle bright*
> *Send the love of friends tonight.*

Place the stone by the candle and leave it there until the
candle burns down. Carry the stone with you for at least a
week.

Love Spell #60: To Turn His/Her Head

Necessary materials:
The foot print of your beloved
Willow tree

Find his/her footprints in the earth, then dig up the dirt or earth that holds the imprint. Take the soil to a willow tree, dig a hole in at its base, and bury the footprint soil and cover it. As you bury the footprint, say:

> *"Many steps on earth there be,*
> *I make my love to think of me.*
> *I am flower, he is stem;*
> *He the cock and I the hen.*
> *Grow, grow big willow tree!*
> *Sorrow the likes of me."*

Love Spell #61: To Gain Forgiveness

Necessary Materials

Paper

Pen

Willow branch or stem of a white rose, thorns and leaves removed.

Jar

Sugar

Write the name of the offended person on one side of a piece of paper, and your name on the other side. Place it, and the stem or branch, into a jar that is filled with sugar. Say:

> *Sugar sweet and sugar pure*
> *Your offense cannot endure.*
> *For your grace now do I plea*
> *that you will learn to forgive me.*

Add water until the jar is almost full and say:

> *With this water I wash away*
> *the anger keeping us away.*

Cap the jar tightly and shake 9 times, saying:

> *Sugar sweet please use your power*
> *Let forgiveness for me flower.*

Shake again nine times. Repeat every day for a week, if need be.

Love Spell #62: Spell to Banish Shyness

Necessary materials:
A garnet
A red candle
A grey candle
A yellow candle.
Musk incense

Cast a circle and light the candles. Light the incense and say three time:

> *Candle one, candle bright*
> *Bring to me my pluck tonight*
>
> *Candle two with candle flame*
> *Never more I'm shy again.*
>
> *Candle three and candle bright*
> *Let the Goddess will tonight.*

Thank the deities you worship and close the circle. Let the candles burn out completely before removing them from the altar.

Love Spell #63: Spell for a Friendship/Love Bond

Necessary Materials:
Pink or white candle
Two pink cups
lemon
jasmine or rose incense
sea salt
athame
permanent pen

This spell is NOT for drawing people unfairly together. It is for strengthening the bond between two or more people.

Open a circle and together declare that the lemon represents your love for each other. Cut away two pieces of the peel, and squeeze the lemon juice into the pink cups. Drink the juice. Then, take the pieces of rind you saved and put them in water. Add the salt, light the incense, and then dry the peels in the flame slightly. Write your name with the pen on the lemon rinds and exchange them. Then, leave the rinds somewhere warm to dry them and then treasure them in a safe place, or wear them around your neck in a bag.

Love Spell #64: Spell for a Love Gone Wrong

Necessary Materials:
Blue pen
Blue piece of paper
9 rose petals
chalice of boiled spring or ocean water
jasmine incense

For best results, perform this on the night before, night of, and the night after a full moon.

Take three rose petals place them in the chalice or cauldron of boiled water. Take your blue paper and write down your concern or problem with the blue pen. Set the cauldron or chalice in an eastern facing window under the light from the full moon, and burn the incense next to the glass. Let sit over night, in the morning pick the rose petals out, add the water to a bath, and bury the rose petals, repeat for each night and after the third night, your problem should begin to work itself out.

Love Spell #65: Wiccan Love Potion Number 9

Necessary Materials:
One pinch of cinnamon
Two teaspoons of cloves
three pinches nutmeg
fresh mint leaves
6 fresh rose petals
6 lime leaves
3 cups pure spring water
brown sugar
honey

For best results, cast this spell on a Friday during a waxing moon.

Place all ingredients in an earthenware or copper tea kettle. Boil three cups of pure spring water and add to the kettle. Sweeten with sugar and honey. Recite this verse:

> *Tonight of nights I brew this tea*
> *To make my beloved desire me*

Drink some of the tea and say:

> *Goddess above please hear my plea*
> *Let [name] desire me!*
> *As you will*
> *So mote it be!*

On the following Friday, brew another pot of the love potion tea and give some to the person you want to love you. If he/she drinks of the tea, he or she will soon begin to fall in love with you.

Love Spell #66: Clove Attraction Spell

Necessary Materials:
Pink Candle
Jasmine Incense
One tablespoon of whole cloves

Light the Jasmine incense, as you do so imagine the kind of person that you want to spend the rest of your life with. Say the qualities that you want in true love out loud as you light the pink candle, and then say this as you place a pile of cloves before the candle as an offering. Say:

> *With incense sweet and candle bright*
> *Bring to me my love to night*
> *Someone honest, loyal, true,*
> *Goddess great I ask of you.*

Blow out the candle, and bury the cloves.

Love Spell #67: Conch Attraction Spell

Necessary Materials:
An Orange candle
Conch shell
Lighter or Matches
Cauldron or bowl
Teaspoon of cinnamon
Silver spoon
Dried rose petals

Light the Orange candle, then take the conch and pass it three times over the flame, as you do this say each time:

> *By power of three*
> *So mote it be*

Take the cinnamon and put it in the bowl. With the spoon, stir it clockwise three times with the Dried Red rose petals. Sprinkle the shell with some of the mixture and imagine yourself glowing with pink energy and vitality. Take the rest of the rose petals and cinnamon mixture and throw it into the wind to carry your request to the God and Goddess. Leave the shell on a windowsill under the light of the moon next time it is full.

Love Spell #68: The Toothpick and Candle Spell

Necessary Materials:
Rose, jasmine, amber, or Night Goddess essential oil
red candle
toothpick
dish

Take a ritual bath with the oil of your choosing. After you emerge, use the toothpick to carve a heart in your candle, and then light the candle and set in a window where there is moonlight.

Put a few drops of the oil on a plate, and say:

> *Toothpick, heart, and candle red*
> *Melt his heart and turn his head.*
> *With this scent I will attract*
> *[name] who I lack.*

Let the candle burn out naturally, then carry the scent with you, spraying on a little whenever you are out or may be meeting people. Increase the power of the magic by repeating the invocation every time you anoint yourself with the scent.

Love Spell #69: Crystal Love Spell

Necessary Materials:
Pink candle
A favorite crystal, charged with your energy.

Light the candle and set it on your altar. Hold the crystal in your left hand and say:

> *Stars are bright and night is black*
> *The one I want I will attract*
> *Goddess great and goddess good,*
> *Bring to me the one who should*
> *Lift my heart and lift my head*
> *Fill my soul and fill my bed.*

Say this three times, and then carry the crystal with you until the next full moon.

Love Spell #70: Love Spell 9

Necessary Materials:
Red or pink candle
Rose or jasmine oil
Silver pin
Red pen
Pink paper

Cast your circle, and take a moment to visualize your ideal mate. After you do so, take the pin and carve the words "love come to me" in the candle.

Then anoint the candle with the oil, starting at the top to center, change hands to do the same from bottom to center. All the while, focus your energy on the candle and envision what you want.

Take the piece of paper and write on it "love come to me" and around the words encircle it with a heart, then set the paper under the candle.

Say aloud:

> *By the gods of hope and truth*
> *By the power of time and youth,*
> *He is mine, his I will be*
> *Lady, send true love to me.*

Take the piece of paper and set it on fire with the candle and repeat the rhyme above, then dismiss the circle.

Love Spell #71: String Love Spell

Necessary Materials:
Rose Incense
Pink candle
Red string
Pink string
White string

After casting your circle, light the candle and the incense and envision the love you would like to attract. You can envision sort of a general idea of what you want, or a specific person. But if you choose to envision a specific person, be sure to say some thing along the lines of: "If we truly are meant to be"

Then, take the 3 strings and braid them together, as you do this, keep picturing your love. When you finish braiding, tie nine knots in it. Tie the chord around your ankle, as by the time it falls off, you should meet your true love.

Love Spell #72: Charred Love Spell

Necessary Materials:
Stick
Lighter
Dried rose petals
White piece Of Paper

Char the end of a stick by holding a lighter to it. As it cools, draw two interlinked hearts onto the paper as you visualize yourself enjoying a relationship. Do not visualize a specific person; just a feeling. Meditate on this for a moment.

Hold the rose Petals in your left hand and charge them with passion. Sprinkle the petals over the linked hearts, and then wrap the paper around the petals. Throw the package into a fire. As it burns, the power is released.

Make sure to only think positive thoughts during this one!

Love Spell #73: Come to Me Love Spell

Necessary Materials:
Red candle
Rose incense
Jasmine incense
Toothpick

Carve the name of the person that you want on the candle, using the toothpick. Light incense, then candle. Burn candle once a day for 10 minutes a day. When the candle is down to an inch, place it on an East-facing windowsill. While doing so visualize your target coming to you as you desire.

Repeat over and over again the following as you visualize your desire and look out the window for at least ten minutes. Say:

> *With the great and rising sun*
> *Bring to me my only love.*
> *Goddess great and goddess kind*
> *Make my true love only mine.*

Love Spell #74: Love Me, Love Me Not Spell

Necessary Materials:
A small, new, red rubber ball
Rose incense

If you like someone but you aren't sure if he/she feels the same way, this is a good way to figure out the truth.

Cast a circle. Light the incense, and then cleanse, consecrate and empower the red rubber ball. Begin bouncing the ball and repeat the following chant:

> *From ground to air, from air to ground*
> *I bounce the magic round and round*
> *Earth and Air, Fire and Water.*
> *My red ball goes higher and higher.*
> *Mine is the magic, mine is the power.*
> *It's time to know the answer*

Repeat the last line as you bounce the ball.

Keep bouncing the ball and say:

> *With harm to none, my will be done.*
> *May this spell not reverse,*
> *or place upon me any curse.*
> *So mote it is!*

You should receive your answer shortly within at least thirty days.

Love Spell #75: Do You Love Me?

This is best done on a Friday. Make sure the moon is waxing. Go to a place where you have a clear view of the moon. Close your eyes and visualize the person you desire. Say:

> *Stars are bright, the moon does glow*
> *Is he in love, I want to know?*
> *Goddess great, give my mind peace*
> *Is he in love, is it with me?*

If the person seems to talk or look at you more often than usual, see this as a sign that he feels love for you. However, be careful with this spell. You must have some reason to believe that the person has feelings for you in the first place for the spell to succeed.

Love Spell #76: Poppet Lust Spell

Necessary Materials:
Picture of intended
Poppet or doll representing intended
Poppet or doll representing you
 Red paper
Red yarn
Three red household candles
Wooden box.
Tape or glue

If you are truly in lust with someone, this is a powerful spell to cast. Make two poppets—one to represent the intended and one to represent you. The poppets don't have to be great works of art; they just have to act as symbols. It's ok to make cardboard cutouts if your arts and crafts skills are too limited to make poppets.

To begin the spell, tape or glue his picture over the doll that represents him, and do the same for the doll that represents you .Write the word "lust" on the red paper, or, if you really want the spell to be more powerful, embroider it into a red piece of cloth with red thread. Tie two knots in the yarn.

Light a red candle for you and a red candle for the target.
Say:

> *Candles flicker while I lust*
> *Have you now I know I must*
> *Flame will burn in candle red*
> *I must have you in my bed.*

Place the target's doll near the target candle and your doll
near yours. Place the third unlit candle between the two
candles. Take the two candles with both hands and light
the center candle with them at the same time. Extinguish
the light of the target candle and your candle.

Cover the dolls facing each other with the cloth and bind
them with the yarn by making one more knot in addition to
the two. Place the dolls in a shoebox and make sure no one
disturbs the box. This should work within a month.

Love Spell #77: Love Enhancer

Necessary Materials:
Pink candle
Toothpick

This should be done at the same hour on seven consecutive Fridays, ending on the one closest to the full moon. Take a pink candle and use the toothpick to carve six rings around it, at equal distances apart. This will give you seven sections of a candle. Light the candle and call out the name of the one you think loves you and say:

> *Goddess great I do implore*
> *I love him/her; make him love me more.*
> *Goddess kind please hear my plea*
> *But as you will*
> *So mote it be.*

Think about the person until the candle has burned dawn to the first line. Then extinguish the candle by snuffing or pinching it, and put it away till next week. On the final week, continue until the candle burns itself out.

Love Spell #78: Bring Someone Close to You

Necessary Materials:
Photo of you
Photo of intended
Silver or porcelain bowl
Pink candle
Rose oil

Take your ritual bath with the rose oil. When you emerge, place the candle in a bowl of water. In front of it, place the photo of you and the photo of your beloved. Light the candle and visualize your love coming to you from far away. Think of your thoughts and his thoughts as pink energy that you can send out to him even if he is halfway around the world.

As you light the candle say:

> *Sacred water flow from me*
> *Endless rivers run to sea*
> *his path to me will now be clear.*
> *He will know his love is here.*
> *His heart will know his journey's end.*
> *In his heart, his soul, his mind,*
> *He'll know he is only mine.*

Let the candle burn until the oil extinguishes it.

Love Spell #79: Affirmation Spell

Necessary Materials:
Two bay leaves
Hair from your head
Hair from head of beloved
Red or pink cloth
Red ribbon

This spell acts as an affirmation between two people in love. It could also be used when making up after a quarrel.

Split the bay leaf in half down the middle. Kneel in front of each other, each holding half the leaf between your hands, which should be palms together as if in prayer.

Hold the leaf halves to your lips and kiss it. Let him do the same with his. Hold your leaf to him, and vice versa, so you can kiss each other's leaves. Hand your half to your partner.

Wrap the hairs around the two halves. Say:

> *With this hair we bind each other*
> *With love and kindness towards the other.*
> *With this hair and leaf of bay*
> *I promise that I will not stray.*

Bundle the hairs and bay leaves together in the fabric, and then tie it with the ribbon.

Do this whenever you feel the need to bond you're your lover.

Love Spell #80: Silver and Crystal Moon Spell

Necessary Materials:
Silver necklace
Pink quartz crystal—preferably as a pendant
Tangerine essential oil

This spell is for meeting a suitable partner.

On the night of a full moon, go outside and stand where you can see it clearly. Rub a few drops of tangerine oil into the crystal. Wear it around your neck. If the crystal is not a pendant, put it in your right hand. Cast your circle of protection, raise both your hands towards the moon and call the moon goddess. Tell her what you want, and what you are looking for. Spend as long as you like experiencing the moon's light. It will charge and empower your spell.

When you have finished, wear the necklace until you are satisfied that you have met someone suitable.

Love Spell #81: Nine Of Hearts Love Spell

Necessary Materials:

A Sheet Of Gold paper

Nine of hearts, either from a normal deck of cards or tarot

A black pen

A box of matches

Bowl

Cast your circle, and when you are ready, write your wish on the Gold paper and wrap it around the nine of hearts.

Burn both items, leaving the ashes in the enamel bowel until your wish has been fulfilled.

Love Spell #82: Papyrus Love Spell

Necessary Materials:
Tablespoon of dried raspberries
Tablespoon of basil
Pinch of Orris root
Two tablespoon rose water or two drops rose essential oil
Small bowl
Paper
Red pen
Red or pink silk

Place the raspberries, basil, Orris root and rosewater into the bowl and mix thoroughly. Cast a circle, and then write the following words onto the paper:

> *The one for whom I always pine*
> *Will change his heart and soon be mine*

Place the paper into the mixture in the bowl, cover it with all the other ingredients and imagine seeing the person you desire. Meditate here for a moment and then take the paper out of the bowl and put it on the red silk. Tie the corners of the red silk together to form a knot.
Charge the bundle with your energy, and carry it with you until you feel the spell working.

Love Spell #83: Holly Love Spell

Necessary Materials:
A Small Branch of Holly
A foot or so of red ribbon
Rose or jasmine oil
Pink candle

This spell is to make a friendship turn into a romantic relationship. Energize the branch of holly and the red ribbon. Imagine your love being reciprocated, and visualize his energy mingling with yours. While putting a few drops of rose oil onto your ribbon, say:

> *Love and passion light our way,*
> *Bring him to me on this day,*
> *Passions burn and hearts desire*
> *Our love born in this candle's fire.*

Set the pink candle in the middle of the altar and light it. Meditate on the flame for a moment. Then wrap the ribbon around the branch and tie it to form three knots. Leave the branch on your altar until you notice a favorable change in your relationship.

Love Spell #84: Cinnamon Spice Spell

Necessary Materials:
Cinnamon
Whole cloves
Red cloth
Red lace
Red candle

This spell will add spice to your love life. Place one tablespoon of the cinnamon powder and one tablespoon in the handkerchief and tie it together using the red lace. Cast a circle and light the red candle.

Holding the handkerchief say:

> *I cast this spell to add some spice*
> *To my love and for my love life*

Repeat three times. Snuff the candle. Place the bag under your bed for as long as you wish.

Love Spell #85: Contact Spell

Necessary Materials:
Small white candle
Photo of lover
Moonstone

This spell is for when you need your partner to contact or reach out to you. Cast a circle, and light the candle. Hold the photograph of your lover in your left hand and repeat:

> *My heart is heavy, my ears ache*
> *For the sound your voice does make.*
> *With this candle, and my stone*
> *I long to you're your dulcet tones.*

Leave the moonstone and the photo on the right side of the altar until you hear from him or her.

Love Spell #86: Amethyst Spell

Necessary Materials:
Piece of amethyst
Photo of you and lover together

This spell will remind your lover of you.

Take your amethyst and charge it with your energy. Wash it in sea salt and water, and as you do so, say:

> *I think of you, you're in my heart*
> *If you think of me, we're not apart.*
> *Hand in hand we make our minds*
> *Our memories and thoughts entwine.*

Then place the Amethyst in front of the photograph and draw a circle of protection around the picture and the piece of amethyst. When you are done, dismiss the circle.

Love Spell #87: Red Heart Spell

Necessary Materials:
White or pink floating candle
Glass or crystal bowl
Spring or ocean water

This spell will help patch up an argument with your lover.

On a Friday night, preferably at midnight, charge all the candles with loving energies and repeat the following while thinking about your lover:

> *Lover mine and lover true*
> *Touch me, thrill me, through and through*
> *Water clear and candles bright*
> *Rekindle our true love tonight.*

Spend a few minutes thinking about the words you have said, then place the candles into the bowl, light them and repeat the above incantation. Imagine you and your lover patching up the argument. Leave the candles to burn out in the water.

Love Spell #88: Lime Tree Love

Necessary Materials:
2 Leaves from a Lime Tree
Tablespoon of honey
Pink candle
White candle
Black pen
Silk bag

This will help you rekindle a dwindling flame.

On the day of a full moon, pick a few leaves from a lime tree and leave them on your altar until the moon is on the wane. On the Friday after the full moon, sit before your altar and cast your circle. Light both candles and, using the black pen, write the name of your lover on one leaf and your name on the other leaf. Then underneath both names, write the words 'reunion' and 'happiness'. Put a drop of honey on one leaf and place the other leaf on top, so that they are pressed together. Energize and charge the leaves with love and passion. Place the leaves in the bag and put the bag under your lover's bed.

Love Spell #89: Coconut Romance Spell

Necessary Ingredients:
One coconut shell, cut in half down the middle
Peach pit
Whole nutmeg
Wild cherry bark
2 tablespoons ginseng
2 tablespoons lemon grass
6 drops of rose oil

This spell will bring romance back into your relationship.

On the night of a new moon, halve all the ingredients and place them into the coconut shells. Using your fingertips, mix the ingredients together in each shell, and charge them with loving, romantic energy.

Meditate with a coconut shell in each hand. Once you feel that you have infused everything with your energy, place the coconut shells in your bedroom, ideally under your bed.

Love Spell #90: Spell for True Love

Necessary Materials:
Purple Candle
Sturdy candle holder
Sharp pencil
Sandalwood or patchouli oil
One rose petal
A Quartz Crystal
A silver bell
A velvet pouch
Matches

Next time the moon is full, place your altar where it will receive the moon's light. Let it stay there. Then at new moon, with the pencil, carve your name on the candle. Rub a drop of oil into your carved name and a drop on the rose petal, and then put the candle in the holder on your altar. Put the rose petal in front of the candle. Hold the quartz crystal in both hands, charging it with energy, and then put the crystal onto the rose petal.

Concentrate and meditate.

When you feel ready, ring the silver bell four times-to summon the energies of Earth, Air, Fire and Water. Light the candle, and sit silently for a moment. Then ring the silver bell three times.

Allow the candle to burn completely. Put the cold candle stub, the crystal and the rose petal into the pouch. Carry this amulet with you to increase the love in your life, and renew the spell on the following new moon.

Love Spell #91: To Make Someone Come To You

Necessary Materials:
Empty reel
Red yarn

When the moon is waxing, take both reels to your altar and sit for a time thinking of all that you want in a partner. Visualize your ideal, and as you do so, begin to wrap the red yarn around the empty reel, effectively transferring the thread from one reel to another. While you are doing this, you should chant the following, continuing throughout the duration of the spell:

> *For my love I wind this thread*
> *So that I may turn his head*
> *I twine the red around the reel*
> *My heart is his alone to steal.*

Once you have transferred all the cotton, put both reels in a safe place and wait for the spell to work.

Love Spell #92: Feather Attraction spell

Necessary Materials:
A feather (preferably peacock) made into a pen
Red ink
A sheet of parchment
A length of red string
A pink candle
Three pink rose petals, dried and crushed
Dragon's Blood powder
An aluminum pan

The person for whom you practice this ritual must already feel a certain attraction for you. This ritual, to some extent, will accentuate the person's feelings for you.

Start by lighting the pink candle. By the light of the candle, take your parchment and write, using the feather pen and red ink, the following incantation:

> *Let so it be that [name] declares his/her love*
> *As the Goddess wills, so mote it be!*

Crush the petals and mix them with the Dragon's Blood, and sprinkle the mixture over each written letter on the parchment. Wait until all is well dried before rolling up the parchment and tying it with the length of string, making three knots. Light the rolled parchment by the flame of the candle and let it burn in the aluminum pan. Repeat the incantation while the parchment is burning.

Love Spell #93: Gypsy Red Spell

The Gypsies say that to find anything red means luck in love. If you find a piece of red thread, red wool, a red button, or whatever, pick it up and carry it with you for luck. It serves as an amulet.

As you stoop to pick it up, think of the person you love and say:

> *"Red is my blood and*
> *red is my heart.*
> *Lucky in love;*
> *Never keep us apart."*

Love Spell #94: Gypsy Drawing Spell

Necessary items:
Amber
Pink or red silk

This should be done on a Friday, first thing in the morning when you rise and before you do anything else. Take a piece of amber and hold it in your (closed) left hand. Hold the hand over your heart, close your eyes, and concentrate your thoughts on the type of person you want to attract to you. See him or her in as much detail as you can. Now kiss the amber and place it in a piece of pink or red silk and wrap it up securely. Carry that with you at all times for the next seven days, sleeping with it under your pillow. Every morning repeat the holding and visualizing, though hold it still wrapped in the silk; don't unwrap it. By the seventh day you will have met someone just like the person you have been wishing for.

Love Spell #95: Spell to Increase Love

Necessary ingredients:
Cauldron
Pink candle
White candle
Red candle
Jasmine incense
Wand

For best results, this should be done during a waxing moon. Place the cauldron on the altar between the pink and the white candles. Inside the cauldron itself, place a red candle. Light love incense and the Pink candles. Tap the cauldron three times with your wand and say:

> *Candle pink I burn to find him*
> *Candle white I burn to bind him.*
> *I now will burn this candle red*
> *To melt his heart and turn his head.*

Tap the cauldron three more times. Light the red candle to speed the spell on its way.

Love Spell #96: Basic Moonstone Love Spell

Necessary Materials:
pink candle
white candle
Cinnamon
Moonstone or rose quartz

Take your ritual bath and then light the candles. Hold one in each hand and visualize pink energy traveling from your hands into the wick, and out to the flame, and then being spread throughout the room.

After a minute or two of doing this, put the candles on the altar, the pink one to the left and the white one to the right. Cast a circle. Place the moonstone or rose quartz on the altar between the two candles.

Next, sprinkle the cinnamon around the two candles. As you sprinkle the cinnamon, speak these words aloud:

> *Goddess of the stars above*
> *Bring to me my one true love!*
> *Goddess great and goddess wise*
> *Bring my true love quickly nigh!*

Snuff out the candle and leave the moonstone or quartz on your altar until you find your love.

Love Spell #97: Circle Love Spell

Necessary materials:
Circular wooden disc
Athame
Honey
Rose oil
Red candle

Take a circular disk, preferably of wood but it can be of cardboard if wood is not possible, and carve a heart into it. Anoint it with rose oil and honey. Take a red candle, any size, light it and let a little of the wax drip onto the heart.

Ask the goddess to show you the true love of your life and then leave the disc face up near a window to symbolize your vigilant watch.

You will soon dream of your lover.

Love Spell #98: Simple Love Spell Number 2

Necessary Materials:
Chalice
Rainwater
Rose petals

Gather rainwater and put it in a consecrated chalice or cauldron. Take this rain inside your house and dab each corner of your bed with a drop. Place rose petals in the water, and sit in the center of your bed.

As you sit say:

> *With the clouds and pouring rain*
> *Bring me love to ease my pain.*

Say this three times, and then take a bath, adding the rainwater to the bathwater.

Love Spell #99: East African Binding Spell

Necessary Materials:
Dish
Pink candle
Chalice or flask of wine
Rose quartz stones
The stem of a rose

Go with your partner to a quiet spot where you can have privacy. You do not necessarily need to be before your altar. Cast a circle and place the candle in its center. Light it. Take a drink of wine from the flask or chalice, which should have been consecrated before beginning.

Make a spacious circle with the rose quartz and stay within that circle. (Moonstone will also suffice.)

Start by looking deeply into the flame, and when you both feel its spirit enter you, walk, skip, or dance clockwise seven times around it.

At the end, pluck a leaf from the rose stem, place it in the dish, and then set it on fire.

As it burns, say

> *Tonight I spend the night with love*
> *Witness to the gods above*
> *Candle candle in the night*
> *As you burn, our love burns bright.*

Drink a toast, and finish the wine if you like.

Love Spell #100: Gypsy Card Spell

Necessary materials:
Deck of cards
Sea salt

Remove from the deck the king, queen, and the five of hearts. At midnight, after a new moon, place the five of hearts over the king and queen. Take a small amount of salt and throw pinches to the four directions as you envision your intended and say:

> *In this deck of cards I place*
> *A wish to see your smiling face.*
> *Pinch of salt and deck of cards*
> *Love of mine, let down your guard.*

Leave the cards in a place where they won't be disturbed. It is said that you will meet each other again by the next full moon.

Love Spell #101: Simple Pink Candle Spell

Necessary Materials:
Pink candle
Rose oil
Orange or tangerine oil

For best results, this should be done on a Friday during a waxing moon.

Hold a pink candle and charge it for future spells by visualizing you and your lover in a loving embrace. Put the energy from this vision into the candle. Anoint the candle in the oils by putting some oil on your index finger, and beginning in the middle of the candle, run your finger to the wick end. Repeat the procedure this time by rubbing the oil from the middle down to the bottom of the candle.

Light the candle and let it burn down completely.

Repeat whenever necessary.

Love Spell #102: Simple Spell for Attraction

Necessary Materials:

Green paper

Ginger root

Earth from the base of a rose bush

Write your name and the intended's name on the paper, put the ginger root and earth in the center of the paper, wrap it up and leave it under your bed. Or, take a piece of parchment paper inscribed with the name of the one you are trying to summon.

The paper is first soaked in ylang ylang oil and then wrapped around the root and tied up with a purple ribbon.

Love Spell #103: To Attract the Attention of The One You Want

Necessary Materials:

Ylang ylang essential oil

Orange pillar candle

Paper

Pen

Glue

Dish

Map showing your home and home of intended

Dress your orange candle in the ylang ylang oil. Write the name of the other person on a piece of paper. Pour some glue onto a dish, and set paper in it, and put the candle on top of it. Light the candle. Cast a circle and say three times:

> *Orange candle, plate and glue*
> *I make myself availed to you.*
> *Orange candle burning bright*
> *Make him think of me tonight.*

Keep the candle burning on the altar until the glue sets completely. While the spell is underway and the candle burns, trace a route on the map from his house to your house. After the candle burns out, put some of the oil on your doorstep. Wear the oil as perfume until the spell has worked.

Love Spell #104: Lust Spell

Necessary materials:
Rose petals
Pink candles
Red candles
Rose oil

Take a ritual bath with pink candles and rose oil. When you emerge, scatter the rose petals in your bedroom, light the red candles, and create a loving vibe in the room. At your altar, light a red pillar candle, anointed with ginger oil, and visualize your lover.

Send loving thoughts to her/him and say:

> *"When we meet, our arms entwine.*
> *When we embrace, our hearts combine.*
> *Passion holds us close together.*
> *Come and kiss me now or never!"*

Now get ready!

For Further reading:

A Reference Guide for the Novice Wiccan, The Ultimate Crash Course in all things Wiccan - Wicca 101
ISBN: 978-1-60332-016-0
By: Kristina Benson

Potions, Incense, Oils & Ointments
ISBN: 978-1-60332-035-1
By: Kristina Benson

Herbalism- A Complete Reference Guide to Frequently used Magickal Herbs, Oils and Spices
ISBN: 978-1-60332-034-4
By: Kristina Benson